ISBN 0 85116 316 5

THE FIRESIDE BOOK

A picture and a poem for every mood
chosen by

DAVID HOPE

Printed and Published by
D. C. THOMSON & CO. LTD.
185 Fleet Street, LONDON EC4A 2HS

BEAUTY

I HAVE seen dawn and sunset on moors and
windy hills
Coming in solemn beauty like slow old tunes of
Spain:
I have seen the lady April bringing the daffodils,
Bringing the springing grass and the soft, warm,
April rain.

I have heard the song of the blossoms and the old
chant of the sea,
And seen strange lands from under the arched
white sails of ships:
But the loveliest things of beauty God ever has
showed to me,
Are her voice, and her hair, and eyes, and the
dear red curve of her lips.

John Masefield

GREEN WOODPECKER

WHEN I were a-coming
   Back home for me tea,
I hears an old yaffle
   Up top of a tree.
And standing beneath him,
   I tries to make out
What that there old yaffle
   Were laughing about.

His cap it were scarlet,
   His jacket were green—
The finest old yaffle
   That ever were seen.
He laughed and he laughed
   As he sat on his bough,
But I couldn't make sense
   Of that yaffle, nohow.

" You silly old yaffle,"
   I started to bawl,
" A-sitting there laughing
   At nothing at all!"
And yaffle, he answered—
   I swear this be true:
" You silly old juggins,
   I'm laughing at you!"

Reginald Arkell

PERFECT FRIENDS

TODAY, my friend Susan arrived on her bike,
   The traffic was bad, so she said.
I admired her new hairdo, the gay-spotted dress,
   The handbag, a bright shiny red.

Relaxing in deck chairs, we sipped lemon tea,
   (It's something she always enjoys),
We chatted of this; we laughed about that
   And deplored the behaviour of boys.

Susan loves apples. The tree in full bloom
   Assures her that all will be well
In the autumn. The herb garden too, she
      approves—
   " Pretty names—and a loverly smell!"

Though Susan's a poppet at four and a half
   And I won't see sixty again,
We're perfect companions, quite sweetly in tune.
   (Tomorrow we're shopping at ten.)

Silvie Taylor

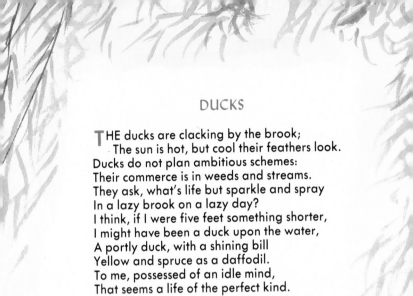

DUCKS

THE ducks are clacking by the brook;
  The sun is hot, but cool their feathers look.
Ducks do not plan ambitious schemes:
Their commerce is in weeds and streams.
They ask, what's life but sparkle and spray
In a lazy brook on a lazy day?
I think, if I were five feet something shorter,
I might have been a duck upon the water,
A portly duck, with a shining bill
Yellow and spruce as a daffodil.
To me, possessed of an idle mind,
That seems a life of the perfect kind.

Clifford Dyment

THE ORCHARD

ALMOND, apple, and peach,
  Walnut, cherry, plum,
Ash, chestnut, and beech,
And lime and sycamore
We have planted for days to come;

No stony monument
But growing, changing things,
Leaf, fruit, and honied scent,
Bloom that the bees explore,
Sprays where the bird sings.

In other Junes than ours
When the boughs spread and rise
Tall into leafy towers
To grace and guard this small
Corner of paradise;

When petals red and white
Resign to warming air,
Without speech or sight
From our hands they will fall
On happy voices there.

Laurence Binyon

I WILL NOT LET THEE GO

I WILL not let thee go.
  Ends all our month-long love in this?
Can it be summed up so,
  Quit in a single kiss?
I will not let thee go.

I will not let thee go.
  Had not the great sun seen, I might;
Or were he reckoned slow
  To bring the false to light,
Then might I let thee go.

I will not let thee go.
  Have we not chid the changeful moon,
Now rising late, and now
  Because she set too soon,
And shall I let thee go?

I will not let thee go.
  Have not the young flowers been content,
Plucked ere their buds could blow,
  To seal our sacrament?
I cannot let thee go.

I will not let thee go.
  I hold thee by too many bands:
Thou sayest farewell, and lo!
  I have thee by the hands,
And will not let thee go.

                              Robert Bridges

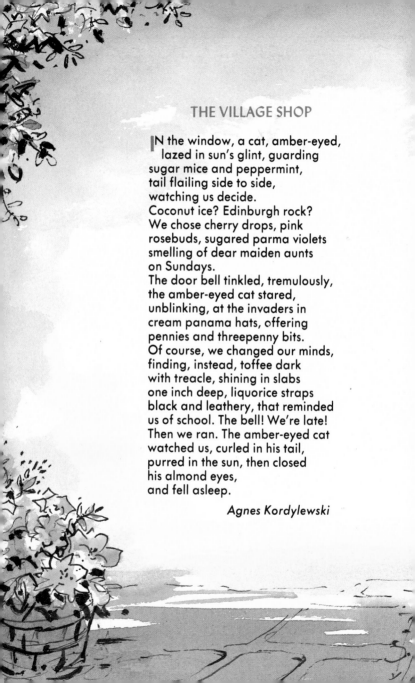

THE VILLAGE SHOP

IN the window, a cat, amber-eyed,
  lazed in sun's glint, guarding
sugar mice and peppermint,
tail flailing side to side,
watching us decide.
Coconut ice? Edinburgh rock?
We chose cherry drops, pink
rosebuds, sugared parma violets
smelling of dear maiden aunts
on Sundays.
The door bell tinkled, tremulously,
the amber-eyed cat stared,
unblinking, at the invaders in
cream panama hats, offering
pennies and threepenny bits.
Of course, we changed our minds,
finding, instead, toffee dark
with treacle, shining in slabs
one inch deep, liquorice straps
black and leathery, that reminded
us of school. The bell! We're late!
Then we ran. The amber-eyed cat
watched us, curled in his tail,
purred in the sun, then closed
his almond eyes,
and fell asleep.

Agnes Kordylewski

IN BRABANT ONCE

I DANCED with you in Brabant once,
   In lighter shoes than these,
With apple blossom on the ground,
   And pink anemones.
Where red mill-sails were turning,
   'Mid colza, grass, and corn,
Where merle and starling fluttered
   In thickets of the thorn.

I danced with you in Brabant once,
   The hauberked knights were there,
Cope and cowl, and chorister,
   And nimbused saints at prayer.
But oh! they never troubled us.
   Among the shining blue
Of larkspur and convolvulus,
   Did not I sit with you?

I know right well the place, milord,
   In little Brabant town,
The sun was shining on your sword,
   And on my silver gown—
The magic and the mystery
   Have long since passed away,
With all the sweet convolvuli
   Of our brief dancing day.

Gloria Rawlinson

THE MEADOW HOLLOW

WHEN young spring calls me I shall haste
    The joys that wait on her to taste,
Where hawthorns with new green are laced,
    Down in the meadow hollow.

The golden lamps of celandine
Out of the ruddled mould shall shine,
And primrose lend her honeyed wine,
    Down in the meadow hollow.

The blackbird and the thrush shall sing,
The blue-tit on the twig shall swing,
And joy break forth from everything,
    Down in the meadow hollow.

The willowed waters sliding by
Shall wash away all mortal sigh;
Oh, who so rich in hope as I,
    Down in the meadow hollow.

John S. Martin

THE NAUGHTY DAY

I'VE had a naughty day today.
　　I scrunched a biscuit in my hair,
And dipped my feeder in the milk,
　　And spread my rusk upon a chair.

When Mother put me in my bath,
　　I tossed the water all about,
And popped the soap upon my head,
　　And threw the sponge and flannel out.

I wouldn't let her put my hand
　　Inside the arm-hole of my vest;
I held the sleeve until she said
　　I really never *should* be dressed.

I crawled along the kitchen floor,
　　And got some coal out of the box,
And drew black pictures on the walls,
　　And wiped my fingers on my socks.

Oh, this *has* been a naughty day!
　　That's why they've put me off to bed.
" He *can't* get into mischief there,
　　Perhaps we'll have some peace," they said.

They put the net across my cot,
　　Or else downstairs again I'd creep.
But, see, I'll suck the counterpane
　　To *pulp* before I go to sleep!

Fay Inchfawn

THE ROSEBUD

QUEEN of fragrance, lovely rose,
    The beauties of thy leaves disclose.
The winter's past, the tempests fly,
Soft gales breathe gently through the sky;
The lark, sweet warbling on the wing,
Salutes the gay return of spring;
The silver dews, the vernal showers,
Call forth a blooming waste of flowers;
The joyous fields, the shady woods,
Are clothed with green, or swell with buds;
Then haste thy branches to disclose,
Queen of fragrance, lovely rose.

Thou, beauteous flower, a welcome guest,
Shalt flourish in the fair one's breast,
Shalt grace her hand, or deck her hair,
The flower most sweet, the nymph most fair.
Breathe soft, ye winds, be calm, ye skies;
Arise, ye flowery race, arise;
And haste thy beauties to disclose,
Queen of fragrance, lovely rose.

But thou, fair nymph, thyself survey
In this sweet offspring of a day.
That miracle of face must fail;
Thy charms are sweet, but charms are frail;
Swift as the short-lived flower they fly;
At morn they live, at evening die:
Though sickness yet awhile forbears,
Yet time destroys what sickness spares:
Now Helen lives alone in fame,
And Cleopatra's but a name:
Time must indent that heavenly brow,
And thou must be what they are now.

This moral to the fair disclose,
Queen of fragrance, lovely rose.

William Broome

ON THE SHORE

I FOUND a little wooden spade
   A-lying in the sand,
And busy footprints to and fro
   Made patterns on the strand.

I found a pail of silver shells,
   A cricket bat and ball,
A castle flying paper flags
   Above her fortress-wall.

A little dog with plashy paws
   Ran barking through the spray
And dropped a pebble at my feet
   Inviting me to play.

And so I walked in secret joy
   Amid a treasure store
Of childhood dreams and memories
   That wait upon the shore.

Betty Haworth

A WARWICKSHIRE SONG

THERE are no oaks in all the shires
   I love so well as those that spill
Smooth acorns from their mailed cups
   Along the Warwick lanes; and still
The Avon holds as clear a way
   As Tweed or Thames, and never blows
The wind along a sweeter land
   Than that where down the Avon goes.

On northern hill and Sussex down,
   In Derby dale and Lincoln fen,
I've trafficked with the winds of God
   And talked and laughed with many men;
I've seen the ploughshare break the earth
   From Cumberland to woody Kent;
I've followed Severn to the sea,
   And heard the swollen tide of Trent.

I know the south, I know the north,
   I've walked the counties up and down,
I've seen the ships go round the coast
   From Mersey dock to London town;
I've seen the spires of east and west,
   And sung for joy at what I've seen,
But oh, my heart is ever fain
   Of ways where Avon's oaks are green.

John Drinkwater

NOD

SOFTLY along the road of evening,
    In a twilight dim with rose,
Wrinkled with age, and drenched with dew,
    Old Nod, the shepherd, goes.

His drowsy flock streams on before him,
    Their fleeces charged with gold,
To where the sun's last beam leans low
    On Nod the shepherd's fold.

The hedge is quick and green with brier,
    From their sand the conies creep;
And all the birds that fly in heaven
    Flock singing home to sleep.

His lambs outnumber a noon's roses,
    Yet, when night's shadows fall,
His blind old sheep-dog, Slumber-soon,
    Misses not one of all.

His are the quiet steeps of dreamland,
    The waters of no-more-pain,
His ram's bell rings 'neath an arch of stars,
    " Rest, rest, and rest again."

Walter de la Mare

PAMPAS GRASS

HOW blows the wind?
    From north to south or east to west?
Whom can I ask who knows it best?

Not the white daisies on the lawn
(Unbidden guests),
For they're so small
They scarcely feel the wind at all.

And liliums shake
   their scented heads, that way and this,
Bemused by wind's caress—
Yet cannot say from whence his kiss.

The chaffinch in the lilac tree
   sings songs to cheer this heart of mine,
But not a jot cares he of how
I hoist my washing on the line.

Fair Cortaderia!
She's the one who knows which way winds blow,
   And which, today, combs out her golden tresses;
Ask her—she'll say!

Mary M. Milne

WELCOME, WILD NORTH-EASTER

WELCOME, wild North-Easter!
　　Shame it is to see
Odes to every Zephyr;
　　Ne'er a verse to thee.
Welcome, black North-Easter!
　　O'er the German foam;
O'er the Danish moorlands,
　　From thy frozen home.
Tired we are of summer,
　　Tired of gaudy glare,
Showers soft and steaming,
　　Hot and breathless air.
Tired of listless dreaming,
　　Through the lazy day:
Jovial wind of winter,
　　Turn us out to play!

Charles Kingsley

A SAXON SONG

TOOLS with the comely names,
  Mattock and scythe and spade,
  Couth and bitter as flames,
  Clean, and bowed in the blade,—
A man and his tools make a man and his trade.

  Breadth of the English shires,
  Hummock and kame and mead,
  Tang of the reeking byres,
  Land of the English breed,—
A man and his land make a man and his creed.

Leisurely flocks and herds,
Cool-eyed cattle that come
Mildly to wonted words,
Swine that in orchards roam,—
A man and his beasts make a man and his home.

Children sturdy and flaxen
Shouting in brotherly strife,
Like the land they are Saxon,
Sons of a man and his wife,—
For a man and his loves make a man and his life.

Victoria Sackville-West

TWO SISTERS

MISS Rosie and Miss Caroline
    Who live on Heather Hill
Are getting on for thirty-nine
    And they are spinsters still.

Miss Rosie loved a travelling man
    Who said, one Autumn day,
" I'm going off to Africa "—
    With that, he went away.

Miss Caroline had loved a priest
    So never could be wed,
For as they say, man cannot live
    Alone by bread.

Miss Rosie scans the atlas
    And Miss Caroline eats cream,
They live each hour of every day
    As if they had a dream

That their old lovers will return—
    So happily—to both,
The travelling man without his map
    The priest without his cloth.

I think at heart the sisters love
    The image—not the men—
They hope to live—they live to hope
    And so Miss Caroline

And Sister Rose of Heather Hill
    The best of both worlds keep,
And as the days go speeding on
    They dream—awake—asleep.

Elizabeth Borland

IN PRAISE OF LONDON

I LOVE Hyde Park, the Serpentine,
  And Marble Arch at half-past nine,
The graceful curve of Regent Street,
The Queen Anne charm of Cheyne Walk
(Its church, with Polyphemus' eye,
And those great chimneys, climbing the sky!)—
The Inns of Court and that discreet
Tavern where Johnson used to talk;
The bustle of Fleet Street and the blare
Of Oxford Circus, Leicester Square;
Charing Cross Road, with books for all
In shop and window, case and stall;

Then who can think of Richmond Hill
In summertime, without a thrill?—
Remembering days with Rose or Nan
When friendship ended, love began,
And glamorous evenings in the park
Under the beech trees hush'd and dark—
The deer that gaze with glistening eyes
The London lights aglow in the skies
(But far away) and no sound there
Save the caught breath and little sighs
That come from joy too great to bear.

Richmond, all London lovers know
Your upland glades, and how, below
The bright Thames twines about your knees
Through the green tracery of your trees . . .
And just as I, on Whitsunday,
Have brought my girl to spend the day,
So to your hill my father came
And, sure, my son will do the same.

Douglas Goldring

PRECIOUS STONES

IF I could choose a perfect stone
  It wouldn't be a costly gem;
Though rubies glow with hidden fire
  They do not speak to me, not them.

The stones I love are ages old,
  Rounded, worn, churned smooth at sea;
Nor do they glint, ice-cold, remote;
  Sun-warmed they are, and facet-free.

From far-flung coves we carried them:
  Brown, smoky-blue and glistening white,
Spoils of the shore for evermore
  To make our garden seaside-bright.

I know of many a patchwork quilt
  Whose little shapes in whispers talk,
But memories sharper still are mine
  When down my pebbled path I walk . . .

Of chubby hands outstretched to show
  The latest treasure, hard to hold.
These sun-kissed beaches everywhere
  Will stay with me when I am old.

Silvie Taylor

IN THE LIBRARY

WHEN with crouched shoulders and attentive
   head
You droop, lovely, above a sullen page,
So ill your eyes expend their wealth of power
Beauty might mourn her wasted heritage:
Yet all the careful wisdom you have read
Lies like the dust upon a thirsty flower.

For I have heard you in clear reveries
Laughing across the Downs, and we have swung
Down Pen-y-Pas together and lain still
On Cleadon when the lark below us sung,
And sunlight rippled to your eager eyes,
And winds went tumbling down the sleepy hill.

Edward Davison

THE TRYST

I SAW her in the crowd one summer day,
  Fresh as a flower as she went her way;
I smiled, and as she glanced in shy surprise
I saw the secret hidden in her eyes.
Then light of step she turned and hastened on
And in a moment eagerly was gone.
Upon the hill that leads into the town
He passed me, young and handsome, striding
    down,
Searching the faces in the crowded street
And in his hand bright flowers for his Sweet.

Betty Haworth

THE BONDSLAVE

WHAT spell was of your weaving
    To take my heart in thrall?
Only a smile, your hand on mine,
    That was all.

What magic did you conjure
    That made my soul your own?
Only the shining of your eyes,
    That alone.

What sign and seal of bondage
    Your gentleness decrees?
A rose to hold, a ring to bind,
    Nought but these.

E. Cawser

AT THE CROSSROADS

THERE is the straight road,
   A long road—
A road that runs to the town.
Full of purpose—important,
Neat-edged and bordered
With hedgerows all ordered.
Cemented and tarred,
Smooth-faced and hard
Is the road that runs to the town.

There is another road,
A steep road—
A road that leads to the farm.
Rutted and grass-grown,
Hedged in with hawthorn,
And perfumed with clover
Is the road that runs over
The fields to the gate of the farm.

But the white road,
A chalk road—
Is the road that leaps to the sea.
Sun-blest and wind-kissed,
Flower-fringed and rain-washed,
Laughing and singing
Is the road that goes swinging
Over the downs to the sea!

Not the straight road,
Or the steep road,
The road that goes to the farm;
But the white road,
The chalk road,
The road that leaps to the sea.
That is the road I am taking,
The road that is calling to me!

Florence Irene Gubbins

THE FIDDLER

MAYBE he has his dreams,
    Frail, as delicate as ours.
To him, perhaps his little travesty of music seems
Gold voice of fire, crowned in one face that gleams
Pale through a mist of flowers,
Shy of the very magic that it brings.
Maybe he builds him palaces and dawn-lit towers
Surging the quiet skies—
The glory of his own imaginings—
For in his own eyes,
Out of his wheezing strings . . .

Maybe he has his dreams,
Strange, yet lovelier than ours . . .

John Anderson

THE TWO LOVERS

A "**H**ER eyes are of a deeper blue
    Than heaven's own celestial hue."
B " I only know, if she were nigh,
  I should not gaze upon the sky."

A " Her face is of a beauty rare
  With which the rose can scarce compare."
B " I only know, if she were close,
  I should not look upon the rose."

A " And when she speaks her voice would pale
  The raptures of the nightingale."
B " I only know, if she were near,
  The nightingale I should not hear."

A " Of any smile from her, the worth
  Is more than heaven, and more than earth."
B " I do not know how that may be,
  But she is heaven and earth to me."

Colin Ellis

CHIMES

BRIEF, on a flying night,
  From the shaken tower,
A flock of bells take flight,
  And go with the hour.

Like birds from the cote to the gales,
  Abrupt—O hark!
A fleet of bells set sails,
  And go to the dark.

Sudden the cold airs swing,
  Alone, aloud,
A verse of bells takes wing
  And flies with the cloud.

Alice Meynell

PICTURES IN THE FIRE

OH, how I love to gather wood,
　　To hear the twig's sharp snap,
The crispling crush of trampled leaves,
The woodpecker's tap-tap-tap.
I thrill to the spine-chilling haunted air
Of the copse in the fading light,
The screech and flap of startled birds,
The vixen's scurrying flight.

And it's captured here in the cheery glow
Of my crackling, cosy fire,
And the witches scream while their
Beady eyes gleam
As the flames leap high'r and high'r:
With their tall peaked caps,
Hissing-spitting black cats
They hold me entranced in a spell,
And the twigs go snap
And the birds flip, flap,
While the red fox springs from the dell.

And oh, how I love the ember glow
When the frenzy dies away
And there's only the old
Black kettle's song
And the clock on the mantle ticking along
And Puss
For company.

Mary M. Milne

IN PRAISE OF WHAT I LOVE

I KNOW a dingle in a leafy wood
   Filled with the fragrance of the perfect May.
Here the grey trees for centuries have stood,
      And Spring wreathes garlands on them, new
      and gay.
Is there a moment of the shining day,
      Fairer than this, which sees the rising sun
Slant the pale yellow of his early ray
      On dew-drenched fallows, and the fine threads
      spun
By long-legged spinners in the clefts of trees,
Float their light gossamer upon the breeze?
Here leaps the limber-footed, listening hare—
And here the cuckoo, blithe and debonair,
      Calls from the willows in the water leas,
Remote, elusive, a thin tongue of air.

Pamela Tennant

A MARCH DAY

THE cock is crowing,
   The stream is flowing,
   The small birds twitter,
   The lake doth glitter,
The green field sleeps in the sun;
   The oldest and youngest
   Are at work with the strongest;
   The cattle are grazing,
   Their heads never raising;
There are forty feeding like one!

   Like an army defeated
   The snow hath retreated,
   And now doth fare ill
   On the top of the bare hill;
The ploughboy is whooping-anon-anon;
   There's joy in the mountains;
   There's life in the fountains;
   Small clouds are sailing:
   Blue sky prevailing;
The rain is over and gone!

William Wordsworth

THE LAST STRAW

*T*ODAY, *my gardener*
  Said to me:
" I often thinks
  Of the likes of we.
You drives a car
  And I rides a bike,
I tries to treat you
  Respectful like!
I comes at eight
  And I leaves at four—
I don't take time
  For me lunch, what's more!
I don't waste time,
  I just jogs along;
I likes to be chivvied
  When I be wrong:
But if you've no time
  For a friendly chat—
You can keep your garden!"
  And that was that.

Reginald Arkell

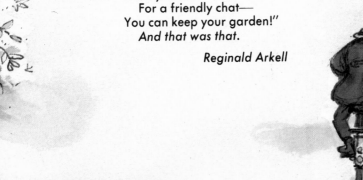

AN OLD GARDEN

LARKSPUR and lavender, hollyhocks gay,
   Catmint and marigold in bright array;
Dahlias and daisies, and sweet-smelling stocks,
Guarded by hedges of neatly clipped box.

Birdsong that wakens the garden at dawn
As, fragrant with dew drops, the new day is born;
Elm trees that whisper as evening draws nigh,
And the first silver stars twinkle down from the sky.

Thank God for gardens, for birds, and for flowers,
Whose goodness decrees that these joys shall be ours;
For what have we done that his love should devise
Such means for poor mortals to glimpse Paradise?

Aileen E. Passmore

THE HAPPY MONTH

BENEATH the green fir branches where doves sit wing to
  wing,
A maid comes up the pathway across the woods of Spring;
Her face is lit with sunshine, her eyes are soft with showers,
Her heart is filled with music and both her hands with
  flowers.

Her tresses touch the beeches, her feet dance in the dew,
And fair about her shoulders the white clouds fleck the
  blue;
Primroses are her fortune and daffodils her care;
Her hand is slipped in Summer's ere half the world's aware.

The last snow fades before her, and looking in her eyes,
Spelled by their witching magic the last rude stormwind
  dies,
And on the cradle branches down all the woodlands deep,
Like a child tired of playing drops suddenly to sleep.

She stands within our garden at breaking of the day,
One hand holds dying snowdrops and one holds budding
  May;
She stands within our garden at falling of the night,
One foot on silver dewdrops and one on hoar frost white.

A month before her coming the thrush to song has thrilled,
A month behind her passing the nesting swallows build;
And this is happy April, fair maid of sun and showers,
With her heart filled with music and both her hands with
  flowers!

Will H. Ogilvie

I DON'T LIKE BEETLES

I DON'T like beetles, tho' I'm sure they're very
    good,
I don't like porridge, tho' my Nanna says I should;
I don't like the cistern in the attic where I play,
And the funny noise the bath makes when the
    water runs away.

I don't like the feeling when my gloves are made
    of silk,
And that dreadful slimy skinny stuff on top of hot
    milk;
I don't like tigers, not even in a book,
And, I know it's very naughty, but I don't like
    Cook!

Rose Fyleman

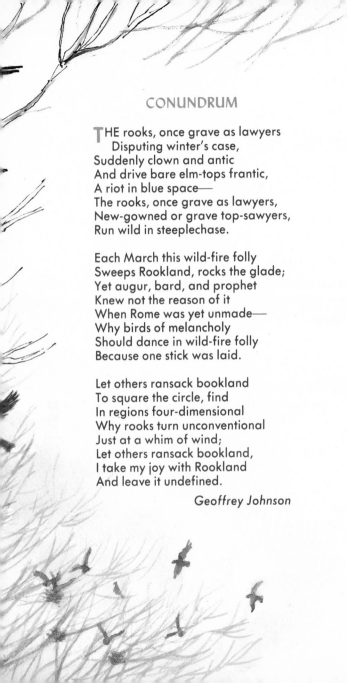

CONUNDRUM

THE rooks, once grave as lawyers
　　Disputing winter's case,
Suddenly clown and antic
And drive bare elm-tops frantic,
A riot in blue space—
The rooks, once grave as lawyers,
New-gowned or grave top-sawyers,
Run wild in steeplechase.

Each March this wild-fire folly
Sweeps Rookland, rocks the glade;
Yet augur, bard, and prophet
Knew not the reason of it
When Rome was yet unmade—
Why birds of melancholy
Should dance in wild-fire folly
Because one stick was laid.

Let others ransack bookland
To square the circle, find
In regions four-dimensional
Why rooks turn unconventional
Just at a whim of wind;
Let others ransack bookland,
I take my joy with Rookland
And leave it undefined.

Geoffrey Johnson

SEA-FEVER

I MUST go down to the seas again, to the
lonely sea and the sky,
And all I ask is a tall ship and a star to steer her
by,
And the wheel's kick and the wind's song and the
white sail's shaking,
And a grey mist on the sea's face and a grey
dawn breaking.

I must go down to the seas again, for the call of
the running tide
Is a wild call and a clear call that may not be
denied;
And all I ask is a windy day with the white clouds
flying,
And the flung spray and the blown spume, and
the sea-gulls crying.

I must go down to the seas again, to the vagrant
gipsy life,
To the gull's way and the whale's way where
the wind's like a whetted knife;
And all I ask is a merry yarn from a laughing
fellow-rover,
And quiet sleep and a sweet dream when the
long trick's over.

John Masefield

A CHARM

TAKE of English earth as much
    As either hand may rightly clutch.
In the taking of it breathe
Prayer for all who lie beneath.
Not the great nor well-bespoke,
But the mere uncounted folk
Of whose life and death is none
Report or lamentation.
    Lay that earth upon thy heart,
    And thy sickness shall depart!

Take of English flowers these—
Spring's full-faced primroses,
Summer's wild wide-hearted rose,
Autumn's wall-flower of the close,
And, thy darkness to illume,
Winter's bee-thronged ivy-bloom.
Seek and serve them where they bide
From Candlemas to Christmas-tide,
    For these simples, used aright,
    Can restore a failing sight.

These shall cleanse and purify
Webbed and inward-turning eye;
These shall show thee treasure hid
Thy familiar fields amid;
And reveal (which is thy need)
Every man a King indeed!

Rudyard Kipling

RAINY NIGHTS

LIKE the town on rainy nights
    When everything is wet—
When all the town has magic lights
    And streets of shining jet.

When all the rain about the town
    Is like a looking-glass,
And all the lights are upside-down
    Below me as I pass.

In all the pools are velvet skies,
    And down the dazzling street
A fairy city gleams and lies
    In beauty at my feet.

Irene Thompson

ECSTASY

I WONDER what they'll think of you and me,
   The poets of a hundred years to come
Who read these words. What will their vision be?
When, fragrant-sweet, straight from some dusty
    tome
Your breathless beauty shines across the years
And colours up the sombre paths of men.
I have you now, 'tis true. I've held you close
Through laughter and through tears. That's why
    my pen
Must make the picture clear for those unborn,
The struggling throng hid in the cave of time.
. . . You are the freshness of the April morn,
The starry splendour of the night sublime,
The quintessence of all that's rich and rare,
The earthly paradise, the heavenly fair.

Haydn Perry

SONG

LOVE, Love today, my dear!
  Love is not always here;
Wise maids know how soon grows sere
The greenest leaf of Spring;
But no man knoweth
Whither it goeth
When the wind bloweth
So frail a thing.

Love, Love, my dear, today,
If the ship's in the bay,
If the bird has come your way
That sings on summer trees;
When his song faileth
And the ship saileth
No voice availeth
To call back these.

Charlotte Mew

ENVOI

EARTH puts her colours by,
    And veils her in one whispering cloak of
      shadow;
Green goes from the meadow;
Red leaves and flowers and shining pools are
      shrouded;
A few stars sail upon a windy sky,
And the moon is clouded.

The delicate music, traced
In and out of the soft lights and the laughter,
Is hushed, round ledge and rafter
The last faint echoes into silence creeping;
The harp is mute, the violins encased,
And the singers sleeping.

So, now my songs are done,
Leave me tonight awhile and the starlight
      gleaming,
To silence and sweet dreaming,
Here where no music calls, no beauty shakes
      me;
Till in my heart the birds sing to the sun
And the new dawn wakes me.

P. H. B. Lyon

ELEGY

MEN who every morning met him,
    Fellows of his daily task,
Pause before they quite forget him.
    " What's become of Jones?" they ask.
And the empty paving-stones
Echo " What's become of Jones?"

Jones has left his native city,
    Stopping not to count the cost.
Spare him, then, a moment's pity,
    You who keep what he has lost.
Jones will never live to be
William Jones, Esq., J.P.

Once we knew, but learned to stifle,
    All the thoughts that turned his brain:
Called security a trifle,
    Counted ease a doubtful gain.
We have learned, as he did not,
To be happy in our lot.

And if once we used to wonder,
    Just before our hair went grey,
If perhaps we made a blunder
    When we signed our souls away
For an income and a wife
And imprisonment for life—

Thoughts like these no more torment us,
    Each delights in all he owns;
Golf and motor-cars content us,
    And the Office. Meanwhile Jones
Leads a life of shift and chance
Somewhere in the South of France.

Colin Ellis

DREAMS

WHEN the grey streets shut me in again in the
    days that come after,
When no more I shall see this blue, glittering sky,
Out of my store-house of dreams I shall take the
    love and the laughter,
The scents and sounds and colour I now lay by.

Oh waves that rock me and love me! Your sun-
    kissed splendour,
Your golden sands, with the frowning cliffs above,
Where the pitiful mosses and grasses and thyme
    creep, starrily tender:
You and the birds about you—you are the friends
    I love.

And when to me you are only dreams in the
    embers—
While you lie wild and forlorn 'neath the wintry
    sky—
Still you may know that the heart of your friend
    remembers:
Wait for me! Wait!—I shall come back again by
    and by.

Thora Stowell

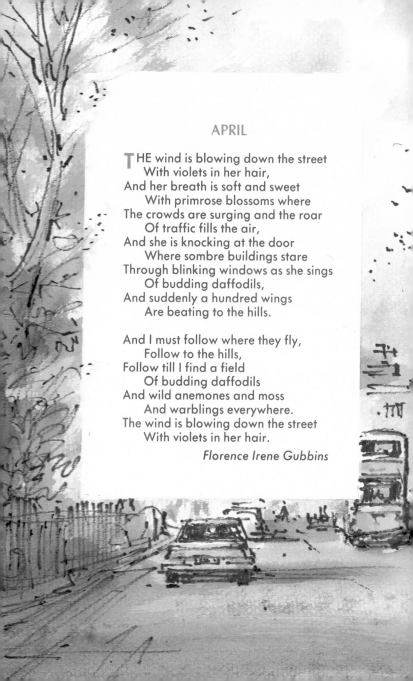

APRIL

THE wind is blowing down the street
    With violets in her hair,
And her breath is soft and sweet
    With primrose blossoms where
The crowds are surging and the roar
    Of traffic fills the air,
And she is knocking at the door
    Where sombre buildings stare
Through blinking windows as she sings
    Of budding daffodils,
And suddenly a hundred wings
    Are beating to the hills.

And I must follow where they fly,
    Follow to the hills,
Follow till I find a field
    Of budding daffodils
And wild anemones and moss
    And warblings everywhere.
The wind is blowing down the street
    With violets in her hair.

Florence Irene Gubbins

WANDERER'S SONG

I HAVE had enough of women, and enough of
   love,
But the land waits, and the sea waits, and day
   and night is enough.

Give me a long white road, and the grey wide
   path of the sea,
And the wind's will and the bird's will, and the
   heartache still in me.

Why should I seek out sorrow, and give gold for
   strife?
I have loved much and wept much, but tears and
   love are not life;

The grass calls to my heart, and the foam to my
   blood cries up,
And the sun shines and the road shines, and the
   wine's in the cup.

I have had enough of wisdom, and enough of
   mirth,
For the way's one and the end's one, and it's soon
   to the ends of the earth;

And it's then good-night and to bed, and if heels
   or heart ache,
Well, it's sound sleep and long sleep, and sleep too
   deep to wake.

Arthur Symons

AFTER THE WAR

NOW to be still and rest, while the heart
   remembers
   All that it learned and loved in the days long
     past,
To stoop and warm our hands at the fallen embers,
   Glad to have come to the long way's end at last.

Now to awake, and feel no regret at waking,
   Knowing the shadowy days are white again,
To draw our curtains and watch the slow dawn
   breaking,
   Silver and grey on English field and lane.

Now to fulfil our dreams, in woods and meadows
   Treading the well-loved paths,—to pause and
     cry
" So, even so I remember it,"—seeing the shadows
   Weave on the distant hills their tapestry.

Now to rejoice in children and join their laughter,
   Tuning our hearts once more to the fairy
     strain,—
To hear our names on voices we love, and after
   Turn with a smile to sleep and our dreams
     again.

Then—with a newborn strength, the sweet rest
   over,
   Gladly to follow the great white road once
     more,
To work with a song on our lips and the heart of
   a lover,
   Building a city of peace on the wastes of war.

P. Hugh B. Lyon

MAY DAY

A DELICATE fabric of bird song
  Floats in the air,
The smell of wet wild earth
  Is everywhere.

Red small leaves of the maple
  Are clenched like a hand,
Like girls at their first communion
  The pear trees stand.

Oh, I must pass nothing by
  Without loving it much,
The raindrops try with my lips,
  The grass at my touch;

For how can I be sure
  I shall see thee again
The world at the first of May
  Shining after the rain?

Sara Teasdale

ESCAPE

SHE called me on the telephone,
   My aging friend who lives alone;
And couldn't hide the wistful note,
But spoke once more of hills remote
Where, fleet of foot and trim of waist,
She'd lived—and loved . . .

I said in haste

(A sudden impulse—mad you'll say—
I'd meant to spend a busy day
With seeds to sow and fruit to freeze,
Blankets washed to catch the breeze)

" Perhaps you'd let me take you there?"
For memories are made to share:

And everything she'd claimed was true;
A magic day we had, we two.

Silvie Taylor

IF I SHOULD EVER . . .

IF I should ever by chance grow rich
  I'll buy Codham, Cockridden, and
    Childerditch,
Roses, Pyrgo, and Lapwater,
And let them all to my elder daughter.
The rent I shall ask of her will be only
Each year's first violets, white and lonely,
The first primroses and orchises—
She must find them before I do, that is.
But if she finds a blossom on the furze
Without rent they shall all for ever be hers,
Codham, Cockridden, and Childerditch,
Roses, Pyrgo, and Lapwater,—
I shall give them all to my elder daughter.

Edward Thomas

SLEEP

I HAVE lived and I have loved;
  I have waked and I have slept;
I have sung and I have danced;
I have smiled and I have wept;
I have won and wasted treasure;
I have had my fill of pleasure;
And all these things were weariness,
And some of them were dreariness.
And all these things, but two things,
Were emptiness and pain:
And Love—it was the best of them;
And Sleep—worth all the rest of them.

Charles Mackay

ACKNOWLEDGMENTS

Our thanks to the Society of Authors as the Literary Representatives of John Masefield for *Beauty* and *Sea Fever;* to the Society of Authors and the Literary Trustees of Walter de la Mare for *Nod;* to Sidgwick and Jackson for *A Warwickshire Song* by John Drinkwater; to Ward Lock Ltd. for *The Naughty Day* by Fay Inchfawn; to Charles Griffiths for *An Old Garden* by Aileen E. Passmore; to Silvie Taylor for *Perfect Friends, Precious Stones* and *Escape;* to P. H. B. Lyon for *Envoi* and *After the War;* to Betty Haworth for *On the Shore* and *The Tryst;* to Mary M. Milne for *Pampas Grass* and *Pictures in the Fire;* to E. Cawser for *The Bondslave;* to Agnes Kordylewski for *The Village Shop;* to Elizabeth Borland for *Two Sisters.*